------< INTERMEDIATE INSIGHTS >-------

Nathan Coppedge

INTERMEDIATE
INSIGHTS

Nathan Coppedge

Nathan Coppedge

INTRODUCTION

This is a collection of thoughts noted for being quotidian. The prodigy here is to produce a plethora of categories, where normally we are accustomed to very few.

Adopting a method somewhere between epiphanic wisdom and everyday fact, the writing becomes challenging. In this case, it is only a challenging writing which merits the attention of readership. That is not to say that it is not eloquent or insightful... It is the quality of boring thoughts which help us think...

It is my aim that this book could be remembered in a similar light to Aristotle's *Scientific Observations* on Nature.

In this book are hints of the Letters of Montaigne and the writings of Lichtenberg. However, efforts were made to be original, to the point of madness...

Nathan Coppedge

INTERMEDIATE INSIGHTS

FIRST, A NOTE:

*---In the following, consider mad-
ness,
Epiphany, prodigy, and science.
That will help you swallow your
medicine---*

*Each thought is highly independent.
Relation is by flow, from
the biggest possible idea of a thing
to the inkling of the next idea---
And then, sometimes, to the
central idea...
of Intermediate Thoughts---*

*Nonetheless, these thoughts come
from a frayed mind, and the mean-
ing is not always as clear as it
should be...*

*As a warning, these 'intermediate
thoughts' may seem extreme to
those that are used to absurdi-
ties...*

Speaking of anthropology,
the dusty smell of the Amtrak
will eventually seem very classic,
In the same way that buses
recall the age of trolleys...

Neanderthals knew the complexity
that picking bones requires teeth,
which are themselves bones.

These thoughts seem quotidian...

Other thoughts are equally com-
plex...

What emerges is what follows...

Nothing is precisely new under the
sun...

Perhaps a schedule may be changed
by a calendar.

An ordinary pattern seems to be
a strewance of bizarre decisions,
all enmattered in the pattern.

We wonder about cold and dreary
days.

But what if the winter is weary?
What if cold is the death of the
day?

Some say brass is not legal tender
anymore. But brass is still valuable.
So this leads to a paradox: brass
coins can simulate exact change.
They might even be of greater
value.

Also, something *stimulates* exact
change---there is something which
is not the coins which evinces the
mechanical transaction...

In general, the weather gives warning even without alarm. There are
ways the weather can be so subtle,
and yet it places the same impor-
tance on things of any caliber...

In some ways, features are softer
years. Who would live with the
headache of all the years one has
lived at once? That would be quite
a pleasurable life!

There are quotidian observations,
which are still profound. Often
these occur in rhymes and word-
play. We can say that bucket icing is
different from cake icing. Unless
you put frosting in a bucket! But,
then again, it was already frosty!
Now what?

People think that semantic thoughts
are thoughts that are too flimsy to
matter. But semantics can equally
apply to very extreme things. We
can say that when women go out,
they don't take a gun. It says nothing, and yet, because of words, it
says everything! Many things must
be like this. Metaphor could be like
this...

There are also things which are not
semantic, which seem profound,
and upon reflection ordinary. Fro-
zen rooms have more mirrors.

There are also seemingly stupid
things which might matter somehow. Spaghetti is thanksgiving.

Some things seem profound only because of difficulty. Shreds of pots
are like shards of pans.

Some things give us an epiphany,
although we're not sure why. And
sometimes we're wrong. A new en-
trance makes two houses.

Some things seem obvious, and also
contradictory. Pretty string is not
pretty bent or broken.

Some things would fool us if it
weren't for our emotional under-
standing. We can be misled
about what we need to believe.
Such as when we say that someone
else is never the same as us.

Nietzsche made a lesser known
statement about causality, saying
that effects are causes. Perhaps
It would be clearer to say, what we
make chooses our choice, no matter
what. When we disagree, then
there is no way to reason about
what the future could mean, is
there?

11

I have thought of a counterpoint to
what Nietzsche said: volition is psy-
chic memory.

Some wonder if Nietzsche was a
metaphysician, and the unstated
answer might be that he couldn't
be while studying philology. But if
he did, he might have wondered,
without trading places, does time
change?

Nietzsche raises a larger question
which is not metaphysics, which is
what is the radical power if it is not
mathematical?

A more common question might be
the koan titled, how do you cheat
at cheating?

Or still more mundanely, okay, who
actually won the football game?

Psychotic poets might wonder about
something more like madness, like
the question of whether reason can
afford anything. What does it do,
make a payment?

Apparently, questioning madness
appears mad.

A break in silence, does it tell the
story of silence?

Is there ever rugged weather
beneath a clear sky?

What parable could a poet moral-
ize, that would make him himself,
and make him a poet?

In truth, does the dark seem more
clear?

Are red roses black in the dark?

Do trees upkeep a surreal house?

Is it not just the sky, but the
weather, which is darker than the
moon?

Are our doors boxes for fear if it
always seems somewhat like
trespassing to go out in public?

13

All an invisible house *is* is invisible.

The mark of a saved man is that he
values a cheap life.

Corrosive bubbles appear to be
hyperbolic. Why don't the bubbles
pop? Or do they? Then how are
they possible? Is it impossible
to prove hyperbole?

Can probability waves absolutely
consist of death and the passing of
time, being as they are, probable,
and consisting in some cases of life
itself?

If a wrinkle in time is an
immortal wink, what is a
wink-wrinkle? This seems
like a humorous problem
with profound consequences...

What is soluble in vision
is not always soluble in space---
Are we racing with the day?
Or is light racing with gravitas?

Can a nude be simplified without
a mind?

What is the question with repeti-
tion? Who would give it a chance?

Who bores a bore? Where is the
homily?

Who needs light tea, also needs water. Bathos, on the other hand, may
be religious without religion.

Glasses are strange to sore eyes.
What could improve them?
Why do glasses seem so strange?
Or is it a sight for sore eyes?

Identities must contract responses,
or by sheer energy, they wouldn't
exist... This seems like a concern
for the metaphysicians...

What number is this 'stage' in
life's theatre? Is there open
grass nearby?

Nathan Coppedge

Infinity keeps going, even when
it doesn't exist. Who would persist
in whatever it is that prevents
life from going?

The senses are strange in a
strange sense? What is stranger
than fiction?

Now for physics: going after matter
has a plan; but how does it matter?

Quandaries emerge, however
ridiculous: What if tongues mat-
tered
like the sun?

Nothing happened every day for
six days, and then something
extraordinary happened on the
seventh day. Is this the day that
you have lived for?

Thought may seem despicable,
if it is always arranging problems.
Acceptance must sound like
an accent...

Some have tried to say, as I say
now, whimsy gives wit rules.

Some insights relate particularly
with our sense of wonder at
nature. The susurrus of a bee's
wing looks like a sunset from
some perspective. Is this
a poem, if poems are about
death? What if the sun is
relatively eternal?

There are also problems in
geometry: if a tree were made
of lines, it wouldn't have lines
in its bark!

Phenomenology has things to say
in that vein: trees are flat to
circular saws.

Traditionally, some of these things
were restrained to fearful exclama-
tions, like 'Cornish hens have bigger
claws'.

My sense of extremities would say
something more like, would a
better place have less grace?

Are answers bones, flesh, or blood?
Being abstract, are they relatively
made of their consequences, in the
body and psyche?

Increase solemnity, and the sense
of just deserts is immense.

Prove a shape.

Salvage a puddle.

The world turns away.

Are the shadows long?

Is life deep?

Are stars crossed?

Do we remember how to sleep?

Is time just what happens when we
hit the wall?

There's something about silver
that is slanted: maybe the way
a puddle looks in the mirror...

Architects have tried to destroy
their own buildings, I presume.
Conscience is great.

Priorities are rarely as great
as merely living.

We are indentured on the past like
the future is indentured on a plan.
With this type of expression, you
can almost see your reflection in
the mirror.

What is merely a surface must be
merely an idea.

Chances are somehow larger than
opportunities.

What if God argues that nothing is
greater than a clock? How would we
disagree? How would we agree?

The world accompanies many abstract thoughts more than it accom-
modates astronauts (this is my be-
lief)---

What is the danger of equivocation
if there is nothing to gain from as-
sertion?

No one really claims the weak
marry the strong...

Fountains give off light in addition
to water. Behold, the sun!

Stoics have said something like:
Nothing is quite as ugly as what is
gone!

What is truly bad must be bad at
everything. Nothing is like that. But
so too, the good must sometimes be
punished.

Impossible things never seem to arrive at breakfast, or we have lost
our patience with the profound!

A dark theatre is the only wolf's clothing I know, unless there are other obtusities...

Pray for lightning and you will make a fine poet or preacher...

Darkness comes to those who fail their will: madness, depression, or merely blissful sleep...

The tunnel out of the clouds is often forgotten...

What makes laughter sleep?

What troubles storms?

What worries words?

Why do we wait for the epiphany of mastery?

Why do we slow when others move past?

Why is the Christian god a scarecrow and a psychopomp?

What worries the worm in the
grass?

What do weeds grow if it is not
weeds? If children are parents, why
aren't they born with seeds?

Aren't habits of mind boring when
defined as such?

What is worse that is worn with
wisdom? What has wisdom that
doesn't age?

Where are the particles that make
everything else? Aren't they too
small to be small?

What is a worrisome course once
it is truly taken? Wisdom booms
and knives still gleam...

Apparently, the world cannot be
worn like a coat...

There is an attitude that binds
'attempt' to 'temptation'. It may
be easiest to consider them disre-
lated, or else go mad.

A storm must be the first kind of
room, because it is the only one
that exists in everyone's classifica-
tion system...

Without reason, roses die. So everyone seems to attest. But roses
aren't the old testament if they
die...

Winters are shaped by a summer of
words. Autumn remembers the
spring.

Sifting is what is really listless...

And nothing endangers the fog...

In some way, people know lightning,
or they regret it when they do,
since regret is a type of memory.

In my mind, nothing flies quite as
straight as a dead horse. That is, if
a fly is the definition of flying.

Arranged marriages die in bed.
But is the bed disarranged? Is the
marriage death, or a mirage, or is
it instead not an arranged marriage?

What is stranger than a night
in a hearse? A night in a car
for the dead?

What worries the weary about the
weak? Is it that they grow more
weary themselves?

Who adopts a flower only to color
it in, they may be a scientist or a
child... Dreams are sometimes writ-
ten very plainly on the brain...

What is the shape of things to
come?

Who is right to cross a bridge?

What is the worry that accompanies
rumination?

What is the pleasure of being born?

Who records reality?

What is the number of stars?

Who records forgetting?

What is an unfinished meal, to
all the animals? Regret, or
prosperity?

Someone knows a famous stone...

What keeps the lunatics awake if
it is not the thought that they are
lunatics?

Who is crosser than a stone?

What worries monks must be out-
side of religion. What about a worrisome monk?

Is touching a stone a kind of opinion
when it is firm?

How do the Joneses keep up with
the Joneses?

No one shares exactly the same
piece of food...

Frequencies seem to travel without
changing their minds.

When does difference arrive with
opinion?

The structure of buildings doesn't
crap bathrooms. Would it be more
or less perverse if it did?

What lightning changes may be
small...

Affording forgets deliberating...

What is primary may be different
from everything else. The politi-
cians know this...

Intangibility is tangible to regret.

No one is quite the same as they
were before...

What once is gone, is somewhat absolute in that way, when that is true.

Seeming is like dreaming, only more abstract.

Roads must be worried about what they are...

Expectation is the physics of meta-physics...

What makes a mother cry some-times frustrates other people...

The glimmer of knowledge escapes obvious answers...

Nothing is trained like a dog with a human name...

Petty differences exude probabil-ity...

What once was the same is now indifferent. Elias Canetti said this.

Shapes seem to perceive whether
they are empty or full. It is their
nature. Sometimes round is a
straight square.

Mathematics ends when the numer-
als are no longer Arabic.

What if we trade in the sun because
the sun is a traitor? Or what if the
sun is the traitor of all traits? Have
I seen the sun? Am I burning?

What is lost is sometimes found. So
what is coherent is not absolute!
At least, not pejoratively...

What makes reason rhyme? An
opposite?

Who doesn't shed their shadow in
the dark? What is the culture that
is not fabulous? On this issue,
innocence is mirth...

Attempts to dream seem boring
when we think lucidity is staying
awake...

Intermediate Wisdom

It is possible to feel relaxed and
wise at the same time.

Good problems are keys to middle
knowledge.

Nathan Coppedge

END OF TEXT

BIO

Nathan Coppedge is previously the author of *"Basic" Platonism* and *How to Write Aphorisms,* as well as many other books. He lives in New Haven, CT.